Fact Finders™

Biographies

Hernán
CORTÉS

by Thomas Streissguth

Consultant:

John P. Boubel, Ph.D.
History Professor, Bethany Lutheran College
Mankato, Minnesota

Capstone
press

Mankato, Minnesota

Fact Finders is published by Capstone Press
151 Good Counsel Drive, P.O. Box 669, Mankato, Minnesota 56002
www.capstonepress.com

Library of Congress Cataloging-in-Publication Data
Streissguth, Thomas, 1958–
    Hernán Cortés / by Thomas Streissguth.
    p. cm.—(Fact finders. Biographies)
    Summary: An introduction to the life of sixteenth-century Spanish explorer Hernán
Cortés, who conquered the Aztec Empire of Mexico.
    Includes bibliographical references and index.
    ISBN 0-7368-2489-8 (hardcover)
    1. Cortés, Hernán, 1485–1547—Travel—Juvenile literature. 2. Mexico—History—
Conquest, 1519–1540—Juvenile literature. 3. America—Discovery and exploration—
Spanish—Juvenile literature. 4. Conquerors—Mexico—Biography—Juvenile literature.
[1. Cortés, Hernán, 1485–1547. 2. Explorers. 3. Mexico—History—Conquest, 1519–1540.]
I. Title. II. Series.
F1230.C835S78 2004
972'.02'092—dc22   2003015258

Editorial Credits
Roberta Schmidt, editor; Juliette Peters, designer; Linda Clavel and Heather Kindseth,
    illustrators; Deirdre Barton and Wanda Winch, photo researchers; Eric Kudalis,
    product planning editor

Photo Credits
Bridgeman Art Library/Index/Museo de America, Madrid, Spain, 11
Corbis/Bettmann, 9, 10, 23; Charles & Josette Lenars, 4–5; Jose Fuste Raga, 6–7
Getty Images/Hulton Archive, cover
Mary Evans Picture Library, 16, 20–21
North Wind Picture Archives, 1, 12–13, 17, 18, 19, 22, 25
Stock Montage Inc., 15

Table of Contents

Chapter 1

Tenochtitlán

On November 8, 1519, Hernán Cortés and his men looked down into a valley. Some of the men thought they were dreaming. A great city was sitting in a large lake. White stone buildings seemed to rise out of the water. Flowers and trees grew everywhere.

Cortés and his men had traveled more than 275 miles (443 kilometers) into what is now Mexico. They had marched over high mountains and through thick forests. They had fought Indians and dangerous animals. Now their journey was over. They were looking down at Tenochtitlán, the capital city of the Aztec **Empire**.

The Aztecs built Tenochtitlán on islands in Lake Texcoco.

Many of the men were worried. They did not know how their small group could **conquer** the great city. But Cortés would not give up. He was ready to take over the Aztec Empire and **claim** the land for Spain.

Chapter 2

A Spanish Beginning

Hernán Fernando Cortés was born in Medellín, Spain, around 1485. His parents were Martin Cortés de Monroy and Catalina Pizarro Altamirano.

Cortés went to the University of Salamanca when he was 14 years old. His parents wanted him to become a lawyer. After two years, Cortés left school. He wanted to **explore** new lands.

Cortés knew the story of Christopher Columbus. When Cortés was about seven years old, Columbus crossed the Atlantic Ocean. Columbus found lands that no Europeans had seen. Cortés wanted to explore this "New World." He left Spain in 1504.

A statue of Cortés stands in Medellín, Spain.

Chapter 3

The New World

Cortés moved to the island of Hispaniola in the New World. He became a farmer. He owned a large area of land and many Indian slaves. But Cortés grew tired of farming. He wanted adventure.

In 1511, Cortés and 300 other men joined an **expedition** led by Diego Velázquez. They traveled to the island of Cuba. They fought the Indians there and took over the island. Velázquez became the **governor** of the island. He gave Cortés land and many Indian slaves. Cortés became a rich and important man in Cuba.

This map shows what Europeans thought the Americas looked like in 1520.

Yucatán

In 1517, Velázquez and Cortés heard about a new discovery. Francisco Fernández de Córdoba found a land west of Cuba. It was called Yucatán. It had gold, silver, and other riches.

Velázquez wanted Yucatán's riches. He decided to send an expedition to this new land. He chose Cortés to be the captain of the expedition.

Cortés left Cuba in 1519 to sail ▼ to Yucatán.

In early 1519, Cortés and more than 500 soldiers sailed to Yucatán. Along the coast, they met Indian groups. Cortés and his men fought with some of the Indians.

Some of the coastal Indians gave women to Cortés as gifts. One of these women was called Malinche. Malinche learned Spanish so she could speak to Cortés and tell him what the Indians said.

Cortés heard from the Indians about a great city in the west. It had gold and many riches. This great city was the capital of the Aztec Empire. The coastal Indians called the city México. The Aztecs called it Tenochtitlán.

Malinche helped Cortés communicate with the Indians.

11

Planning the Conquest

Cortés told his men that they would become rich and famous. They only had to help him conquer the Aztec Empire. Cortés then destroyed their ships. Without a way to leave, the men had to go with him. In August 1519, Cortés and his men started the journey to Tenochtitlán.

Cortés destroyed the ships so his men could not leave.

On the way to Tenochtitlán, many Indians joined Cortés and his men. These Indians did not like the Aztecs. They wanted to help Cortés fight the Aztecs. By the time they reached the capital city, Cortés was leading more than 20,000 men. But Cortés' army was small compared to the city's population. Nearly 1 million Aztecs lived in Tenochtitlán.

Chapter 4

The Aztecs

Cortés and his men reached Tenochtitlán on November 8, 1519. They received a warm welcome as they entered the capital city. Several hundred Aztec nobles went out to greet them.

At the gates of the city, Cortés saw Montezuma, the **emperor** of the Aztecs. The emperor was about 50 years old. He wore robes made of feathers and pearls. His sandals were decorated with gold.

Cortés got off his horse and stepped forward to meet Montezuma. Cortés put a necklace around the emperor's neck. Cortés told him he came as a friend, not as a conqueror. Cortés was lying.

Montezuma welcomed Cortés as a friend.

15

Some historians say that Montezuma believed Cortés was the Aztec god Quetzalcoatl. According to old Aztec stories, this god had a white face and a dark beard. Cortés arrived the same year Quetzalcoatl was supposed to return.

Montezuma was put in chains and made a prisoner.

Cortés learned about Tenochtitlán and the Aztecs. He was amazed at the great city. But he did not like the Aztec religion. The Aztecs believed human blood was a great gift to their gods. The Aztecs killed and **sacrificed** thousands of people each year.

Cortés decided to take over the city. He made Montezuma his **prisoner**. Cortés made himself the ruler.

Trouble

In April 1520, Cortés heard that Velázquez, the governor of Cuba, was upset with him. Cortés was not supposed to conquer the Aztecs. Velázquez sent an army to stop Cortés.

Cortés and about 120 men left Tenochtitlán to meet the army. Cortés led a surprise attack. After the battle, Cortés gave gold to the army and told the men about the Aztecs. Many of the men decided to help Cortés conquer the Aztecs. More than 1,000 Spaniards marched back to Tenochtitlán.

The army sent by Velázquez surrendered to Cortés.

▲ The Aztecs
trapped the
Spanish inside
the palace.

Cortés found trouble when he
returned to Tenochtitlán. The man he
left in charge had killed many Aztecs.
The angry Aztecs trapped Cortés and
his men inside the palace.

Cortés asked Montezuma to talk to
the Aztecs. Montezuma tried, but they
threw stones at him. One stone hit
Montezuma on the head. He died
from the wound.

La Noche Triste

On June 30, 1520, Cortés and his men tried to escape from Tenochtitlán. During the night, they started to sneak across the bridges to the mainland. Before they reached land, the Aztecs attacked them. Many men died during the battle.

Cortés and about 400 Spaniards made it to land. They called that night *la noche triste*, the sad night.

Cortés and his men went to the villages of the friendly Tlaxcala Indians. They rested there for nine months. They also gathered more people for an attack on the Aztecs.

▲ The Aztecs attacked when the Spanish tried to escape.

FACT!

Many men drowned during *la noche triste*. They were weighed down by their armor and the gold they had taken from the palace.

Chapter 5

The Conquest

On December 26, 1520, Cortés led 25,000 men to Tenochtitlán. They built small boats and took over the lake around the city. Cortés now controlled the island city. No one could get in or out.

Many Aztecs died during the following months. Some died because they ran out of food. Others died from smallpox or other **diseases**. Cortés and his men had unknowingly brought these European diseases to the Aztecs.

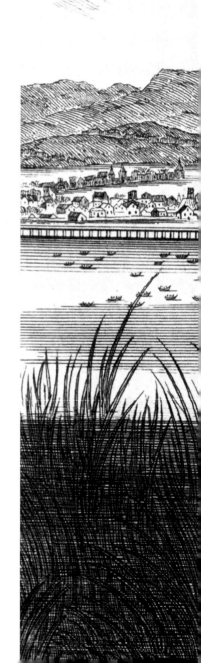

The Spanish took control of Lake Texcoco and trapped the Aztecs in Tenochtitlán.

The Spanish and the Aztecs fought over Tenochtitlán for more than two months.

The Battle of Tenochtitlán

On June 9, 1521, Cortés started to attack the city. The battle was long and hard. The Aztecs had a brave new leader. He was Montezuma's nephew, Cuauhtémoc. Week after week, Cuauhtémoc led the Aztecs against Cortés and his army.

Cortés soon realized that he had to destroy Tenochtitlán. He had to get rid of the Aztecs' hiding places. Cortés' men burned all of the buildings. The beautiful city was reduced to ashes.

The battle lasted more than two months. Thousands of people died. On August 13, Cortés caught Cuauhtémoc. The battle ended. Cortés had conquered the Aztec Empire.

The Battle of Tenochtitlán ended when Cuauhtémoc ▼ was captured.

Chapter 6

After the Conquest

Cortés became the governor of the conquered land. The land became part of what Europeans called New Spain. Cortés built a new city on top of Tenochtitlán. He called it Mexico City.

Cortés went to Spain in 1528. The king named him captain general of New Spain. Cortés returned to New Spain the following year.

Cortés continued to explore new lands. In 1535, he sailed to what is now Baja California. Cortés sent other men to explore the Pacific Ocean and lands that later became Guatemala and Honduras.

In 1540, Cortés went back to Spain. He died there on December 2, 1547.

In Spain, Cortés was welcomed as a hero.

Lasting Impact

New Spain was one of the most important Spanish **colonies** in the New World. It was also one of the largest. The colony had large amounts of gold and silver. It had plenty of good land to farm. Thousands of Spanish colonists sailed across the Atlantic Ocean to settle in New Spain. Hundreds of new towns and cities were built in the plains and mountain valleys. Much of New Spain later became known as Mexico.

Cortés' conquest of Mexico was one of the most important events in history. Mexico's resources made Spain one of the richest and most powerful countries in Europe. In return, Spain changed Mexico. The Spanish language and many Spanish customs became a part of Mexico's culture.

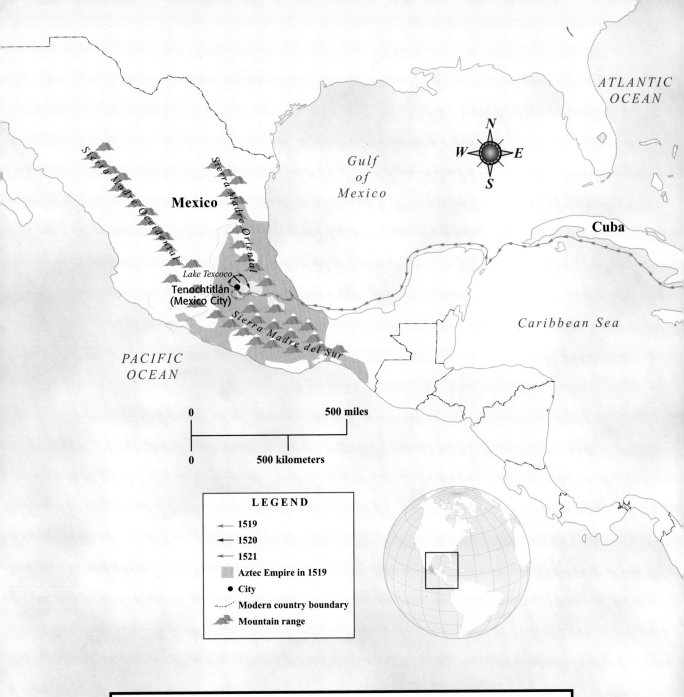

ATLANTIC
OCEAN

*Gulf
of
Mexico*

Mexico

Sierra Madre Occidental

Sierra Madre Oriental

Lake Texcoco

Tenochtitlán
(Mexico City)

Sierra Madre del Sur

Cuba

Caribbean Sea

*PACIFIC
OCEAN*

N
W E
S

0 ⟶ 500 miles

0 ⟶ 500 kilometers

LEGEND

⟵ 1519
⟵ 1520
⟵ 1521
▨ Aztec Empire in 1519
● City
⋯ Modern country boundary
▲ Mountain range

The Journeys of Hernán Cortés, 1519–1521

Fast Facts

- Cortés grew up in southwestern Spain.

- After Cortés moved to the New World, he helped take over the island of Cuba.

- In early 1519, Cortés went to Yucatán to find gold. He heard about the great riches in a city called México or Tenochtitlán.

- In November 1519, Cortés went to Tenochtitlán and took over the city.

- The Aztecs forced Cortés and his army out of the city on *la noche triste*. Cortés stayed with friendly Indians until he was ready to attack the Aztecs again.

- In 1521, Cortés conquered Tenochtitlán and the Aztec Empire. He claimed all of the land for Spain.

- Cortés named the land New Spain. Today, the land is called Mexico.

Time Line

Life Events of Hernán Cortés

Hernán Cortés is born in Medellín, Spain.

Cortés conquers the Aztecs and wins Mexico for Spain.

Cortés helps Diego Velázquez conquer Cuba.

Cortés dies in Spain on December 2.

1485 1492 1507 1511 1519–1521 1522 1531–1534 1547

World Events

Christopher Columbus crosses the Atlantic Ocean.

Ferdinand Magellan's ship *Victoria* returns to Spain. It is the first ship to sail around the world.

The western continents are named after Amerigo Vespucci. They become known as North America and South America.

Francisco Pizarro conquers the Incas and wins Peru for Spain.

29

Glossary

claim (KLAYM)—to say that something belongs to you or that you have a right to have it

colony (KOL-uh-nee)—an area that has been settled by people from another country; a colony is ruled by another country.

conquer (KONG-kur)—to defeat and take control of an enemy

disease (duh-ZEEZ)—a sickness or illness

emperor (EM-pur-ur)—the male ruler of an empire

empire (EM-pire)—a large territory ruled by a powerful leader

expedition (ek-spuh-DISH-uhn)—a long journey for a certain purpose, such as exploring

explore (ek-SPLOR)—to travel to find out what a place is like

governor (GUHV-urn-ur)—a person who controls a country or state

prisoner (PRIZ-uhn-ur)—a person who is held by force

sacrifice (SAH-kruh-fyess)—to offer something to a god

Internet Sites

FactHound offers a safe, fun way to find Internet sites related to this book. All of the sites on FactHound have been researched by our staff.

Here's how:
1. Visit *www.facthound.com*
2. Type in this special code **0736824898** for age-appropriate sites. Or enter a search word related to this book for a more general search.
3. Click on the **Fetch It** button.

FactHound will fetch the best sites for you!

Read More

Crisfield, Deborah. *The Travels of Hernán Cortés.* Explorers and Exploration. Austin, Texas: Steadwell Books, 2000.

DeAngelis, Gina. *Hernando Cortés and the Conquest of Mexico.* Explorers of New Worlds. Philadelphia: Chelsea House, 2000.

Kline, Trish. *Hernán Cortés.* Discover the Life of an Explorer. Vero Beach, Fla.: Rourke, 2003.

Index